A Season *for* Simplicity

paintings by Donny Finley

Harvest House Publishers
Eugene, Oregon

A Season *for* Simplicity

Copyright © 1999 by Harvest House Publishers
Eugene, Oregon 97402

ISBN 0-7369-0108-6

Artwork designs are reproduced under license from © Arts Uniq'®, Inc., Cookeville, TN and may not be reproduced without permission.
For information regarding art prints featured in this book, please contact:

Arts Uniq'
P.O. Box 3085
Cookeville, TN 38502
800-223-5020

Design and production by Koechel Peterson & Associates, Minneapolis, Minnesota

Harvest House Publishers has made every effort to trace the ownership of all poems and quotes. In the event of a question arising from the use of a poem or quote, we regret any error made and will be pleased to make the necessary correction in future editions of this book.

Scripture quotations are taken from The Living Bible, Copyright © 1971 owned by assignment by Illinois Regional Bank N.A. (as trustee). Used by permission of Tyndale House Publishers, Inc., Wheaton, Illinois 60189. All rights reserved; from the New American Standard Bible, © 1960, 1962, 1963, 1968, 1971, 1972, 1973, 1975, 1977 by The Lockman Foundation. Used by permission; and from the Holy Bible, New International Version®, Copyright © 1973, 1978, 1984 by the International Bible Society. Used by permission of Zondervan Publishing House.

Printed in Hong Kong

00 01 02 03 04 05 06 07 08 /IM/ 10 9 8 7 6 5 4 3 2

*L*et your boat of life be light, packed with only what you need—a homely home and simple pleasures,

one or two friends worth the name, someone to love and someone to love you…

~

JEROME K. JEROME

Oh, Lord, I thank you for the privilege and gift of living in a world filled

with beauty and excitement and variety. I thank you for the gift of loving

and being loved, for the friendliness and understanding and beauty

of the animals on the farm and in the forest and marshes,

for the green of the trees, the sound of a waterfall, the darting beauty

of the trout in the brook. I thank you for the delights of music and children,

of other men's thoughts and conversations and their books to read

by the fireside or in bed with the rain falling on the roof

or the snow blowing past outside the window.

~

LOUIS BROOMFIELD

IT IS THE SIMPLE THINGS OF LIFE THAT MAKE LIVING WORTHWHILE,
THE SWEET FUNDAMENTAL THINGS SUCH AS LOVE AND DUTY,
WORK AND REST AND LIVING CLOSE TO NATURE.

LAURA INGALLS WILDER

5

The ability to simplify means to eliminate the unnecessary

so that the necessary may speak.

~

HANS HOFMANN

They say a person needs just three things to be truly happy in this world.

Someone to love, something to do, and something to hope for.

~

TOM BODETT

MY RICHES CONSIST NOT IN THE EXTENT OF MY POSSESSIONS,
BUT IN THE FEWNESS OF MY WANTS.

J. BROTHERTON

SOMEONE *to* LOVE,

SOMETHING *to* DO,

and SOMETHING *to* HOPE FOR

Let us learn to be content with what we have.

Let us get rid of our false estimates, set up all the higher ideals—

A quiet home,

Vines of our own planting,

A few books full of the inspiration of genius,

A few friends worthy of being loved and able to love in return,

A hundred innocent pleasures that bring no pain or remorse,

A devotion to the right that will never swerve,

A simple religion empty of all bigotry, full of trust and hope and love—

and to such a philosophy this world will give up all the joy it has.

~

DAVID SWING

YOU HAVE LET ME EXPERIENCE THE JOYS OF LIFE AND THE
EXQUISITE PLEASURES OF YOUR OWN ETERNAL PRESENCE.

THE BOOK OF PSALMS

VINES *of* OUR *own* PLANTING

Happy the man whose wish and care

A few paternal acres bound,

Content to breathe his native air

In his own ground.

Whose herd with milk, whose fields with bread,

Whose flocks supply him with attire,

Whose trees in summer yield him shade;

In winter, fire.

~

ALEXANDER POPE

OUR LIFE IS FRITTERED AWAY BY DETAIL. SIMPLICITY, SIMPLICITY, SIMPLICITY!

HENRY DAVID THOREAU

The weary Mole also was glad to turn in without delay, and soon had his head

on his pillow, in great joy and contentment. He saw clearly how plain

and simple…it all was; but clearly, too, how much it all meant to him,

and the special value of some such anchorage in one's existence…

it was good to think he had this to come back to, this place which was all

his own, these things which were so glad to see him again and could always

be counted upon for the same simple welcome.

~

KENNETH GRAHAME
THE WIND IN THE WILLOWS

12

FORGET NOT TO SAY OFTEN,
I HAVE ALL I HAVE EVER ENJOYED.
MRS. L.M. CHILD

Preserve *the* Heart *and* Secure Comfort

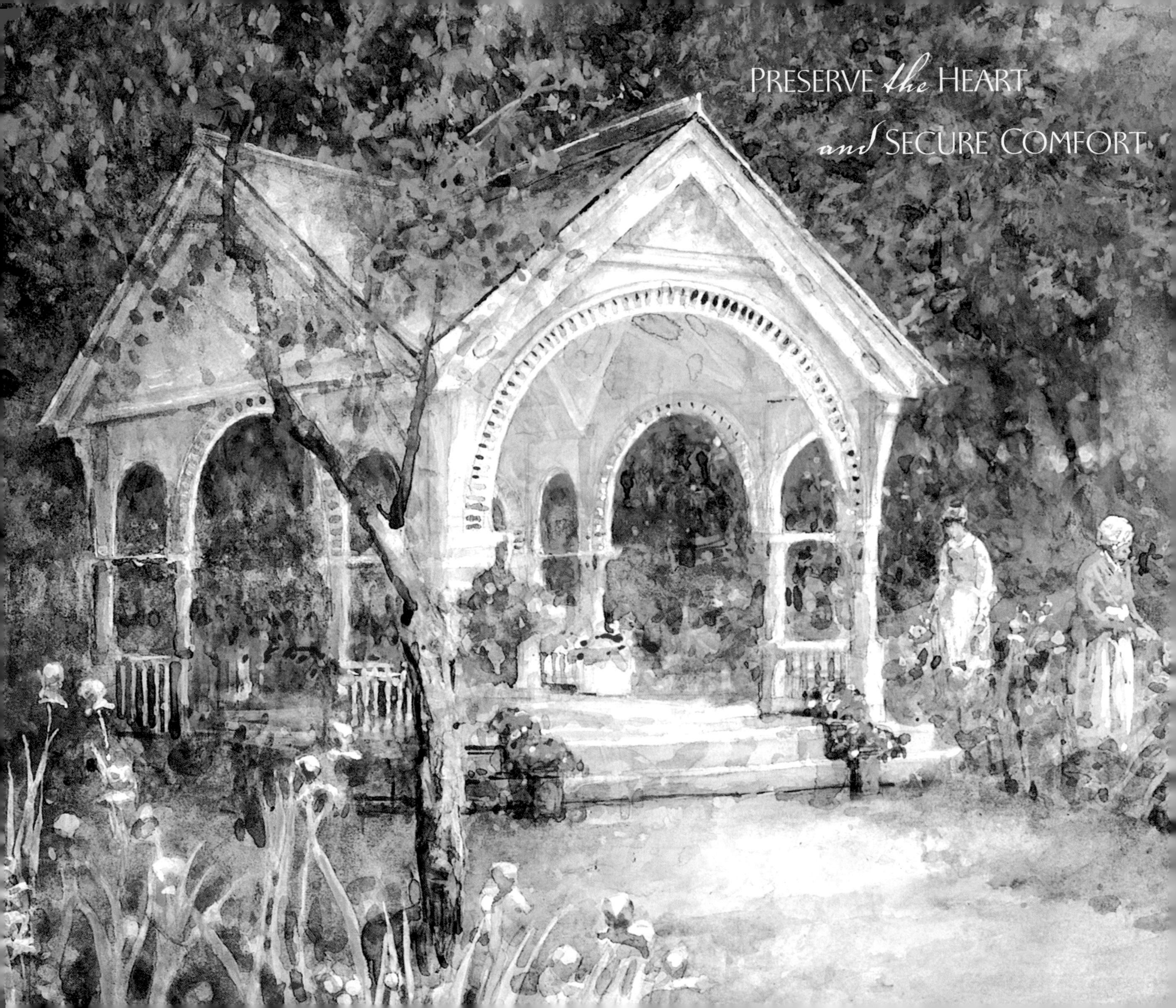

Then it was that Jo...learned to see the beauty and the sweetness of Beth's nature,

to feel how deep and tender a place she filled in all hearts,

and to acknowledge the worth of Beth's unselfish ambition to live for others,

and make home happy by that exercise of those simple virtues which all may possess,

and which all should love and value more than talent, wealth, or beauty.

~

LOUISA MAY ALCOTT
LITTLE WOMEN

15

LIFE IS MADE UP, NOT OF GREAT SACRIFICES OR DUTIES, BUT OF LITTLE THINGS,
IN WHICH SMILES AND KINDNESS, AND SMALL OBLIGATIONS GIVEN HABITUALLY,
ARE WHAT PRESERVE THE HEART AND SECURE COMFORT.

SIR H. DAVY

Not much from this great world I ask

Beyond the strength to do my task.

It is enough that I may be

On hand to see a blossoming tree

And hear a songbird, now and then,

Singing his hymns of joy to men.

Books on a shelf; a ruddy fire,

A restful nook whene're I tire;

Laughter of children at their play,

Outside a little garden gay,

Where all the blazing summer through

Comes into bloom some splendor new.

I do not ask that life shall be

Forever care and sorrow free,

Nor that some distant morning I

Shall not awake to grieve and sigh.

I ask but faith to stand before

Whate'er the future has in store.

Let me be one whose courage springs

From all the countless little things

Of joy and beauty which abound

Wherever man may look around.

Let me exult in peace or strife

That I have had the gift of life.

EDGAR A. GUEST

the BEST THINGS *are* NEAREST

isn't the big pleasures that count the most;

it's making a great deal out of the little ones.

~

JEAN WEBSTER

he best things are nearest: breath in your nostrils,

light in your eyes, flowers at your feet, duties at your

hand, the path of God just before you.

~

ROBERT LOUIS STEVENSON

ALWAYS LOOK OUT FOR THE SUNLIGHT THE LORD SENDS INTO YOUR DAYS.

HOPE CAMPBELL

True happiness arises, in the first place, from the enjoyment of one's self,

and in the next, from the friendship and conversation

of a few select companions.

~

JOSEPH ADDISON

20

A FIERY SUNSET, TINY PANSIES BY THE WAYSIDE, THE SOUND OF RAINDROPS
TAPPING ON THE ROOF—WHAT AN EXTRAORDINARY DELIGHT TO SHARE
SIMPLE WONDERS WITH A TRUE FRIEND!

HEATHER HARPHAM KOPP

*V*ery little is needed to make a happy life. It is all within

yourself, in your way of thinking.

MARCUS AURELIUS

A man's life does not consist in the abundance

of his possessions.

THE BOOK OF LUKE

NOW AND THEN IT'S GOOD TO PAUSE IN OUR PURSUIT
OF HAPPINESS AND JUST BE HAPPY.

GUILLAUME APOLLINAIRE

PAUSE *in* OUR PURSUIT *of* HAPPINESS

and JUST *be* HAPPY

WHERE *your* HEART,
THERE *your* HAPPINESS

*G*od grant that I may live upon this earth

And face the tasks which every morning brings

And never lose the glory and the worth

Of humble service and the simple things.

~

EDGAR A. GUEST

25

*W*e live in deeds, not years; in thoughts,

not breaths; in feelings, not figures on the dial;

we should count time by heart-throbs.

~

PHILIP JAMES BAILEY

WHERE YOUR PLEASURE IS, THERE IS YOUR TREASURE; WHERE YOUR TREASURE,
THERE YOUR HEART; WHERE YOUR HEART, THERE YOUR HAPPINESS.

AUGUSTINE

Live your life each day as you would climb a mountain.

An occasional glance toward the summit keeps the goal in mind,

but many beautiful scenes are to be observed from each new vantage

point. Climb slowly, steadily, enjoying each passing moment;

and the view from the summit will serve

as a fitting climax for the journey.

~

HAROLD V. MELCHERT

27

WE GATHER SIMPLE PLEASURES LIKE DAISIES BY THE WAY.

LOUISA MAY ALCOTT

Laura was very happy.

The wind sang a low, rustling song in the grass.

Grasshoppers' rasping quivered up from all the immense prairie.

A buzzing came faintly from all the trees in the creek bottoms.

But all these sounds made a great, warm, happy silence.

~

LAURA INGALLS WILDER
LITTLE HOUSE ON THE PRAIRIE

28

TEACH US TO DELIGHT IN SIMPLE THINGS...

RUDYARD KIPLING

Joys Come *from* Simple *and* Natural Things

*N*ature is beautiful, always beautiful!

Every little flake of snow is a perfect crystal,

and they fall together as gracefully as if fairies of the air

caught water drops and made them into artificial flowers

to garland the wings of the wind!

~

MRS. L.M. CHILD

*N*ature gives to every time and season some beauties of its own;

and from morning to night, as from the cradle to the grave,

is but a succession of changes so gentle and easy that we can

scarcely make their progress.

~

CHARLES DICKENS

JOYS COME FROM SIMPLE AND NATURAL THINGS:
MISTS OVER MEADOWS, SUNLIGHT ON LEAVES,
THE PATH OF THE MOON OVER THE WATER.
SIGURD F. OLSON

To live as gently as I can;

To be, no matter where, a man.

To take what comes of good or ill

And cling to faith and honor still;

To do my best and let that stand—

The record of my brain and hand;

And then, should failure come to me,

Still work and hope for victory.

To have no secret place wherein

I stoop unseen to shame or sin;

To be the same when I'm alone

As when my every deed is known;

To live undaunted, unafraid

Of any step that I have made;

To be without pretense or sham

Exactly what I think I am.

To leave some simple mark behind

To keep my having lived in mind;

If enmity to aught I show,

To be an honest, generous foe,

To play my little part, nor whine

That greater honors are not mine.

This I believe, is all I need

For my philosophy and creed.

EDGAR A. GUEST

In character, in manner, in style, in all things,

the supreme excellence is simplicity.

~

HENRY WADSWORTH LONGFELLOW

We urge you to…make it your ambition to lead

a quiet life and attend to your own business

and to work with your hands…

~

THE BOOK OF 1 THESSALONIANS

Peace does not dwell in outward things,

but within the soul…

~

FENELON

34

WHAT SWEET DELIGHT A QUIET LIFE AFFORDS.

WILLIAM DRUMMOND

the SUPREME EXCELLENCE

is SIMPLICITY

I love the little joys of life—

The smell of rain, the sound of brooks,

The taste of crispy toast and jam,

The sight of rows and rows of books.

~

REBECCA MCCANN

*N*o entertainment is so cheap as reading,

nor any pleasure so lasting.

~

LADY M.W. MONTAGUE

*T*he man whom neither riches nor luxury nor grandeur

can render happy may, with a book in his hand,

forget all his troubles under the friendly shade of every tree,

and may experience pleasures as infinite as they are varied,

as pure as they are lasting, as lively as they are unfading,

and as compatible with every public duty as they

are contributory to private happiness.

~

ZIMMERMANN

THE LOVE OF READING ENABLES
A MAN TO EXCHANGE THE
WEARISOME HOURS OF LIFE,
WHICH COMES TO EVERYONE,
FOR HOURS OF DELIGHT.

MONTESQUIEU

37

'Tis the gift to be simple

'Tis the gift to be free

'Tis the gift to come down where we ought to be

And when we find ourselves in the place just right

'Twill be in the valley of love and delight.

When true simplicity is gain'd,

To bow and to bend we shan't be ashamed.

To turn, turn will be our delight

'Till by turning turning we come round right.

When true simplicity is gain'd,

To bow and to bend we shan't be ashamed.

To turn, turn will be our delight

'Till by turning turning we come round right.

~

SIMPLE GIFTS

Life is a gift to be used every day,

Not to be smothered and hidden away;

It isn't a thing to be stored in the chest

Where you gather your keepsakes and treasure your best;

It isn't a joy to be sipped now and then,

And promptly put back in a dark place again.

Life is a gift that the humblest boast of,

And one that the humblest may well make the most of;

Get out and live it each hour of the day,

Wear it and use it as much as you may;

Don't keep it in niches and corners and grooves—

You'll find that in service its beauty improves.

EDGAR GUEST

LIFE *is a* GIFT *to be* USED *every* DAY

do EVERYTHING QUIETLY

and IN *a* CALM SPIRIT

The attributes of a great lady may still be found in the rule of the four S's:

Sincerity, Simplicity, Sympathy and Serenity.

EMILY POST

Never be in a hurry; do everything quietly and in a calm spirit.

Do not lose your inward peace for anything whatsoever,

even if your whole world seems upset. Commend all to God,

and then lie still and be at rest in His bosom.

ST. FRANCES DE SALES

43

OCCUPY THYSELF WITH FEW THINGS, SAYS THE PHILOSOPHER,
IF THOU WOULDST BE TRANQUIL.

MARCUS AURELIUS

Nothing is more simple than greatness; indeed,

to be simple is to be great.

~

RALPH WALDO EMERSON

But, as you know, my heart is usually brimful of happiness.

The thought that my dear Heavenly Father is always near,

giving me abundantly of all those things which truly enrich my life

and make it sweet and beautiful, makes every deprivation seem of little moment

compared with the countless blessings I enjoy.

~

HELEN KELLER

TODAY A NEW SUN RISES FOR ME; EVERYTHING LIVES...
EVERYTHING INVITES ME TO CHERISH IT.

ANNE DE LENCLOS

to BE SIMPLE

is to BE GREAT

To be glad of life because it gives you the chance to love

and to work and to play and to look up at the stars;

to be satisfied with your possessions, but not contented with yourself

until you have made the best of them; to despise nothing in the world

except falsehood and meanness, and to fear nothing except cowardice;

to be governed by your admiration rather than your dislikes;

to covet nothing that is your neighbor's except his kindness of heart

and gentleness of manner; to think seldom of your enemies,

often of your friends, and every day of Christ…

~

HENRY VAN DYKE

NOTHING BETTER FOR A MAN THAN THAT HE SHOULD EAT AND DRINK,
AND THAT HIS SOUL SHOULD ENJOY GOOD IN HIS LABOR.

THE BOOK OF ECCLESIASTES

Simplicity is making the journey of this life with just baggage enough.

~

CHARLES DUDLEY WARNER